LITERATURE RESPONSE LOGS

Reproducible Prompts for Every Day

by
Barbara L. Rentschler
Sandra Lee Schuler

Good Apple

To Melody Nichols,
a constant source of inspiration and encouragement,
and the dedicated staff at Grasse Elementary

Good Apple
A Division of Frank Schaffer Publications, Inc.
23740 Hawthorne Boulevard
Torrance, CA 90505-5927

Editor: Susan Eddy

1 2 3 4 5 6 7 8   MAL   01 00 99 98

PREFACE

Several years ago, when our sixth-grade reading program moved from basals to trade books, we organized a reading workshop using self-selected trade books. Students were taught reading skills and strategies in large- and small-group settings. Uninterrupted Sustained Silent Reading (USSR) occurred daily for at least 30 minutes. During that time, teachers and trained volunteers conducted book conferences.

Students were asked to complete books and prepare for conferencing every two weeks. To meet this obligation, they used the USSR period at school and assigned reading time at home. On the due date, students submitted their books and conferences were scheduled. They then chose new reading selections and began another two-week cycle.

We found we needed new procedures to manage our reading workshop because there were as many different books being read as students in class. We wanted a simple method of tracking student progress and monitoring interactions with fictional text. We visualized a tool that could be completed by every student, regardless of book choice. Our goal was to activate thinking in each reader before, during, and after reading.

To meet our needs, we designed weekly reading logs with a prompt for each day of the week. Our first attempts produced highly satisfactory results—the new tool did accommodate the diverse reading choices of our students. We could track their book selections, their reading rates, and their ability to process and interact with text. Complex thinking was activated by prompts that focused on story grammar, literary techniques, and life experiences. We decided to integrate subject areas with literature, assigning each curriculum to a day or days of the week:

- **MONDAY**—language arts and fine arts
- **TUESDAY**—science
- **WEDNESDAY**—math
- **THURSDAY**—social studies and affective domain
- **FRIDAY**—language arts and fine arts

Unfortunately, within one marking period, we found ourselves recycling the same prompts!

When starting new books, students frequently had difficulty responding to prompts because they had not read enough. Since in our workshop books were due every other Wednesday, we assigned math prompts to that day. (Most math entries could be completed with minimal reading.) However, some students completed books ahead of schedule and started new ones on other days of the week. If these readers could not respond to the daily prompt, they were given three options: answer the prompt after reading at home, answer a prompt for a different day, or write a one-sentence summary and place a star in the left margin of the log.

We have refined the reading logs over five years and have created prompts for every day of the school year. Our goals were to have students connect literature with other curricula and their lives by using higher-order thinking skills. The benefits for teachers are many.

- We can quickly monitor reading progress and assess concept development in reading and other curricular areas.

- We can use student responses to choose appropriate mini-lessons in reading and other curricular areas.

- We can document independent work habits by following entries of book titles, reading times, and page counts.

Students sequence and file their work throughout the school year using the number at the top of each log. This format enables students to organize their work, chart their progress, and make selections for their portfolios.

The logs can be used in many settings, including small-group literature discussions, whole-class reading assignments, or discussions about a read-aloud book. They can be used with basals or in other curricular areas to begin or end a class.

INTRODUCTION

Getting Started

To achieve the best results when using these reading logs, it helps to communicate a sense of their value to students. Explain that through responding to these prompts, students can reveal themselves daily as investigators, decision-makers, problem-solvers, predictors, and inventors. Feel free to model concise, well-developed responses so that students can demonstrate the critical- and creative-thinking skills needed to fill these roles.

Teacher Preparation

Each prompt in *Literature Response Logs* is unique. Search the collection for ones that meet your needs and the abilities of your students. Second-language learners, for example, may need to have figurative expressions and idioms explained before working independently or with a partner.

When using logs with a read-aloud book, select those that do not require students to scan the text for specifics. To emphasize the importance of responding in complete sentences, choose logs eliciting that kind of response. If you want students to apply learning in one subject area to another, scan the collection for prompts that will meet your objective.

In the upper right corner of each log is a frame in which you may record the number of each log as it is used. The logs can then be filed in sequence for future reference. The numbering allows you to track and monitor reading progress.

Student Preparation

Introduce reading logs with a read-aloud book. Number a log and distribute copies to the class. Display a copy or project it onto a screen. Point out the basic information required at each reading. Guide students as they enter the book title, starting time, and beginning page number. Ask students to read the day's prompt with you. Remind them to consider this question as you read aloud. After reading, enter the time you finished and the page number on which you stopped. Have students follow your example. (See Figure 1.)

Name __Mimi Connell__   **READING LOG**   __1__

MONDAY: Book __Morning Girl__
Time __9:45-10:15__   Pages __11 - 26__
Examine the first paragraph of your book. Does the author focus on the
characters, the setting, or an event? _____
Copy phrases that support your answer.
_____
_____

Direct students to respond in complete sentences unless the prompt states otherwise. On a transparency or on the chalkboard, share several possible answers to the prompt. Explain that log entries can be labeled powerful, satisfactory, or inadequate. (See the appendix.) Ask them to rate the samples. Help students identify attributes of a powerful response. Direct them to reread and rate their responses. Encourage revisions that will make the entries powerful.

On the second day, share powerful responses you found among students' log entries. Review the attributes of a powerful response. Then repeat the steps taken the previous day. On the third day, guide the class through the procedure again. Pair students with partners to rate each other's responses. Each should help the other with revisions.

Maintenance

After three guided sessions, most students will be ready to work independently. Those who are having difficulty should be given extra support individually or in a small group.

To encourage and maintain excellence in responses, share powerful student examples on a regular basis. Lots of exposure helps students recognize and construct powerful answers. Invite students to add their best responses to their portfolios.

Recycling specific logs will help you and your students assess growth in specific areas and should be considered when appropriate. Encourage students to create original logs for future classroom use as well.

Name _____   # READING LOG ___

MONDAY: Book _____
Time _____ Pages _____
Examine the first paragraph of your book. Does the author focus on the
characters, the setting, or an event? _____
Copy phrases that support your answer.

_____

_____

_____

TUESDAY: Book _____
Time _____ Pages _____
Scientists classify animals according to certain characteristics. On the
back of this paper classify two characters by their most noticeable traits.
Provide phrases from the text that support your classification.

_____

_____

_____

WEDNESDAY: Book _____
Time _____ Pages _____
Math involves recognizing patterns. Books also contain patterns.
Describe a pattern in your story.

_____

_____

THURSDAY: Book _____
Time _____ Pages _____
Archaeologists find and interpret artifacts to study different cultures.
What artifact would help you understand the characters in your story? _____
Explain. _____

_____

_____

FRIDAY: Book _____
Time _____ Pages _____
Suppose you are making your book into a movie and you need to
select background music. Describe the music you would choose for
the part you read today. Defend your choice.

_____

_____

_____

Name _____   # READING LOG   [____]

MONDAY: Book _____

Time _____   Pages _____

Write a one-sentence summary of what happened in today's reading.

_____

_____

_____

_____

TUESDAY: Book _____

Time _____   Pages _____

Choose a specimen from your story that you would like to examine more closely.

_____

Explain why you chose this specimen.

_____

_____

_____

WEDNESDAY: Book _____

Time _____   Pages _____

Divide the number of days you have to complete this book into the number of pages you have to read. How many pages must you read per day to meet the deadline? _____
Show your work on the back of this paper.

THURSDAY: Book _____

Time _____   Pages _____

Uniforms are worn by doctors, nurses, firefighters, police officers, and others. What uniform would best fit the behaviors of the main character?

_____

Explain. _____

_____

_____

_____

FRIDAY: Book _____

Time _____   Pages _____

What would be the perfect gift for the main character? _____

Explain. _____

_____

_____

© 1997 Good Apple

READING LOG

___

MONDAY: Book _____

Time _____ Pages _____

A compound sentence contains two complete phrases. Write a compound sentence that describes how you chose the book you are reading.

_____

_____

_____

TUESDAY: Book _____

Time _____ Pages _____

What weather condition describes today's reading? _____

Explain. _____

_____

_____

WEDNESDAY: Book _____

Time _____ Pages _____

Estimate the number of words in the last paragraph you read today. _____

Count the number of words in that paragraph. _____

Find the difference. _____

THURSDAY: Book _____

Time _____ Pages _____

Compare and contrast yourself with the main character in your book.

Jot down your notes in the Venn diagram below.

_____

_____

_____

_____

_____

_____

FRIDAY: Book _____

Time _____ Pages _____

Write a newspaper headline that summarizes the section you read today.

_____

_____

Name _____

READING LOG ____

MONDAY: Book _____

Time _____ Pages _____

From whose point of view is this story told? _____

Is it told in the first person or in the third person? _____

Describe where and when the story takes place.

_____

_____

Ask a partner or a group member to check your answer and initial. _____

TUESDAY: Book _____

Time _____ Pages _____

Think about your main character's personality.

What animal do you think would be most like him or her? _____

Explain. _____

_____

_____

WEDNESDAY: Book _____

Time _____ Pages _____

Is your main character more like an equilateral, isosceles, or scalene triangle?

Give reasons to support your answer.

_____

_____

_____

THURSDAY: Book _____

Time _____ Pages _____

People belong to groups based on interests, talents, backgrounds, or beliefs.

In what kind of group would your character belong? _____

Explain. _____

_____

_____

FRIDAY: Book _____

Time _____ Pages _____

List four adjectives that describe your character's appearance or personality.

1. _____ 3. _____

2. _____ 4. _____

Name _____   # READING LOG _____

MONDAY: Book _____

Time _____ Pages _____

Suppose the main character filled out a job application.
What special skills could that person list?

_____

_____

_____

TUESDAY: Book _____

Time _____ Pages _____

Some animals change their behavior in different surroundings.
How does your main character change in different surroundings?

_____

_____

_____

WEDNESDAY: Book _____

Time _____ Pages _____

How many pages are in your book? _____
If the whole book equals 1, write a decimal number that names
the approximate amount of pages you have read. _____

THURSDAY: Book _____

Time _____ Pages _____

Select a family member who is most like a character in your story.
Explain how the two are alike.

_____

_____

_____

FRIDAY: Book _____

Time _____ Pages _____

Choose a paragraph and read it aloud to a partner. Why did you choose that paragraph?

_____

_____

_____

Partner's initials and comments

_____

_____

Name _____   # READING LOG ____

MONDAY: Book _____

Time _____ Pages _____

Many readers decide whether they like a book after reading the first two pages.

Assign a letter grade to the first two pages of your book. _____

Explain the grade.

_____

_____

_____

TUESDAY: Book _____

Time _____ Pages _____

Plants and animals depend on each other for food and energy.

Explain how two characters in your book depend on each other.

_____

_____

_____

WEDNESDAY: Book _____

Time _____ Pages _____

Find a math-related situation from your book, such as one involving
distance or the cost of items. Use the information in a word problem
that requires an estimated quotient. Remember to include the answer.

_____

_____

_____

THURSDAY: Book _____

Time _____ Pages _____

On the back of this paper draw a map that shows the setting of the story.

FRIDAY: Book _____

Time _____ Pages _____

Name an activity at which you know you could beat your main character.

_____

Explain why you would be the winner.

_____

_____

_____

Name _____

READING LOG

MONDAY: Book _____

Time _____ Pages _____

Create a three-box flowchart on the back of this piece of paper. In each box, write
a recent event from your book. Make sure they are in the correct sequence.

TUESDAY: Book _____

Time _____ Pages _____

Sound can be produced by hitting, plucking, stroking, or blowing.
Write a sentence from your reading today that has sound.

_____

_____

How was the sound produced?

_____

_____

WEDNESDAY: Book _____

Time _____ Pages _____

Determine the approximate age of each main character in your story.
Order them from youngest to oldest.

_____

_____

THURSDAY: Book _____

Time _____ Pages _____

If you went shopping with your main character,
what kind of store would that person want to visit?

_____

Explain.

_____

_____

FRIDAY: Book _____

Time _____ Pages _____

What subject would your main character enjoy the most at school?

_____

Explain.

_____

_____

Name _____   # READING LOG ___

MONDAY: Book _____

Time _____   Pages _____
Write a story summary using present-tense verbs.

_____

_____

_____

TUESDAY: Book _____

Time _____   Pages _____
Landforms are natural features of the land, such as mountains and coastlines.
What landform is near or part of the story setting?

_____

How might the story change if the landform changed?

_____

_____

WEDNESDAY: Book _____

Time _____   Pages _____
Using facts from your story, write and solve a math word problem that requires
either multiplication or division. Show your work on the back of this paper.

_____

_____

THURSDAY: Book _____

Time _____   Pages _____
Identify a story character's value or belief. _____
How does that character act on that value or belief?

_____

_____

FRIDAY: Book _____

Time _____   Pages _____
Examine the book's cover and title. What effect might they have on a reader?

_____

Did they help you choose to read the book? _____
Explain.

_____

_____

16

Name _____

READING LOG ____

MONDAY: Book _____

Time _____ Pages _____

A simple sentence contains a complete subject and predicate. Write a simple sentence that summarizes today's reading. Draw a vertical line to separate the subject from the predicate. Underline the simple subject and circle the simple verb.

_____

_____

TUESDAY: Book _____

Time _____ Pages _____

Interesting writing appeals to the reader's sense of taste, smell, touch, hearing, or sight. To which sense does the author appeal in your story at this time?

_____

How do you know?

_____

_____

_____

WEDNESDAY: Book _____

Time _____ Pages _____

How many pages are in your book? _____

Circle the decimal that best represents how much you have read:

    0.25   **0.50**   **0.75**   **1.0**

Use a calculator to find the correct amount. Write the amount in decimal form.

_____

THURSDAY: Book _____

Time _____ Pages _____

A *rebus* represents words or syllables with pictures whose names are similar. Invent a rebus that summarizes today's reading. Draw it on the back of this paper.

FRIDAY: Book _____

Time _____ Pages _____

Synergy comes from an ancient Greek word that means "working together." Between which two characters is there synergy?

_____

What do they do together?

_____

_____

_____

Name _____   # READING LOG ⬜

MONDAY: Book _____

Time _____ Pages _____

Write a summary sentence that has a compound subject naming two story
characters. The predicate of the sentence should describe what they are doing.

_____

_____

TUESDAY: Book _____

Time _____ Pages _____

Grease and oil reduce friction between a machine's moving parts. What could
reduce friction between two story characters who are irritated with each other?

_____

Explain. _____

_____

_____

WEDNESDAY: Book _____

Time _____ Pages _____

A *simile* is a figurative phrase that compares two unlike things, using the

word *like* or *as*. Complete this simile: The main character, _____,

is like a rectangle because

_____

_____

THURSDAY: Book _____

Time _____ Pages _____

Brainstorm two nicknames for your main character that describe that person's personality.

1. _____   2. _____

Circle the nickname you like better and explain why.

_____

_____

FRIDAY: Book _____

Time _____ Pages _____

If you were to inhabit the body of the main character for a day, what would you gain?

_____

What would you lose?

_____

_____

18

Name _____

READING LOG _____

MONDAY: Book _____

Time _____ Pages _____

Describe the main character of your story in a sentence that has a linking
verb (such as the word *is* or *was*) followed by at least two adjectives.

_____

_____

_____

TUESDAY: Book _____

Time _____ Pages _____

Magnets attract various objects.

What object attracts a character in your story? _____

How can you tell?

_____

_____

_____

WEDNESDAY: Book _____

Time _____ Pages _____

Sometimes people make bets with others.

What might be a bet for your main character to make?

_____

_____

What are the odds that he or she would win the bet? _____

THURSDAY: Book _____

Time _____ Pages _____

Describe a story problem that is important to all people, not just the characters in the story.

_____

_____

_____

FRIDAY: Book _____

Time _____ Pages _____

Writers often choose precise words that help readers visualize the story.

Describe an event from your story that you can clearly picture in your mind.

_____

_____

_____

READING LOG ____

MONDAY: Book _____

Time _____ Pages _____

A compound sentence contains two complete phrases.
Summarize today's reading using a compound sentence.
One of the phrases should include a compound subject.

_____
_____
_____

TUESDAY: Book _____

Time _____ Pages _____

On the line below, name a story character whose traits make that
person seem transparent, translucent, or opaque. Circle your answer.

_____ Transparent? Translucent? Opaque?

Explain. _____
_____
_____

WEDNESDAY: Book _____

Time _____ Pages _____

On the back of this paper, create a line graph that shows the number
of pages you have read each day since you began your book.

THURSDAY: Book _____

Time _____ Pages _____

Describe how an event in the book has affected two story characters in different ways.
Name both characters in your answer.

_____
_____
_____
_____

FRIDAY: Book _____

Time _____ Pages _____

Write a one-word summary of today's reading. _____

Compare your answer with a partner's. Explain how they are alike and different.

_____
_____
_____

Name _____

READING LOG _____

MONDAY: Book _____

Time _____ Pages _____

A declarative sentence ends with an exclamation point.

Write a declarative sentence that explains the main character's problem.

_____

_____

TUESDAY: Book _____

Time _____ Pages _____

Healthy people usually eat low-fat foods and exercise regularly.

Is your main character healthy? _____

Explain. _____

_____

_____

WEDNESDAY: Book _____

Time _____ Pages _____

How many pages are in your book? _____

On what page did you stop reading today? _____

A *proper fraction* is a fraction that represents an amount less than one.

Write a proper fraction that tells what part of the book you have read.

_____

_____

THURSDAY: Book _____

Time _____ Pages _____

Choose a setting from your story that is similar to your community.

Describe how they are alike.

_____

_____

_____

FRIDAY: Book _____

Time _____ Pages _____

Pretend the main character is your secret pal in a book exchange.

What would be the perfect book to give? _____

Why? _____

_____

Name _____   # READING LOG _____

MONDAY: Book _____

Time _____ Pages _____

Suppose you are the main character.

What do you predict you will do on the next three pages?

_____

Check your prediction later. Was it correct? Explain.

_____

_____

TUESDAY: Book _____

Time _____ Pages _____

Light is important when using a microscope.

What object in your story would you like to examine under a microscope?

_____

Explain. _____

_____

_____

WEDNESDAY: Book _____

Time _____ Pages _____

Find a mathematical term in the section you read today.

Tell whether it did or did not have a mathematical meaning.

Term _____   Did   Did Not

Explain. _____

_____

_____

THURSDAY: Book _____

Time _____ Pages _____

Suppose your story occurred in another land about 100 years earlier.

Describe one event in your book that could not occur and explain why.

_____

_____

FRIDAY: Book _____

Time _____ Pages _____

Write a two-sentence summary of what happened in today's reading.

_____

_____

Circle the common nouns in your sentences. Underline the proper nouns.

Name _____ # READING LOG _____

MONDAY: Book _____

Time _____ Pages _____

An author uses alliteration when he or she writes a group of words
that share the same initial sound. Create an alliterative title for your book.
Make the initial sound match that of the main character's name.

Main character _____

Title _____

TUESDAY: Book _____

Time _____ Pages _____

Atoms form chemical bonds by giving or receiving electrons.
People and animals form bonds by sharing common experiences.
Choose two characters in your book and explain their bond.

_____

_____

WEDNESDAY: Book _____

Time _____ Pages _____

Guess the age of the oldest character in your story. _____

What story clues support your guess?

_____

_____

THURSDAY: Book _____

Time _____ Pages _____

Suppose you want to trade for a personal possession of the main character.

What would it be? _____

What might the character like in return? Why?

_____

_____

_____

FRIDAY: Book _____

Time _____ Pages _____

What type of music do you think the main character in your story prefers—

classical, country, soft rock, heavy metal? _____

Explain. _____

_____

_____

Name _____

MONDAY: Book _____

Time _____ Pages _____

Study the beginning of your book.
What one sentence makes you want to complete the story?

_____

_____

Explain your choice.

_____

_____

TUESDAY: Book _____

Time _____ Pages _____

Use weather terms to forecast tomorrow's reading.

_____

Check your prediction tomorrow. Was it correct? Explain.

_____

WEDNESDAY: Book _____

Time _____ Pages _____

Write a recipe on the back of this paper that would produce a being just like the
main character. List the ingredients and the quantities, then tell how to combine them.
Give the recipe a title that includes the character's name.

THURSDAY: Book _____

Time _____ Pages _____

If you could peek into the main character's treasure box,
what one thing might you find?

_____

Why do you think it is important to the character?

_____

_____

FRIDAY: Book _____

Time _____ Pages _____

What action verb best describes the action in today's reading?

_____

Explain, using story details.

_____

_____

Name _____ # READING LOG ___

MONDAY: Book _____
Time _____ Pages _____
How would the story change if the characters and their problems
were moved to a ship or to another planet?

_____
_____

TUESDAY: Book _____
Time _____ Pages _____
In his work with pea plants, Gregor Johann Mendel formulated an
understanding of dominant and recessive genes.

What character is dominant in your story? _____

Recessive? _____

Explain. _____

_____
_____

WEDNESDAY: Book _____
Time _____ Pages _____
What mathematical symbol best describes today's reading? _____
Explain. _____

_____
_____

THURSDAY: Book _____
Time _____ Pages _____
In what time period is your story written: before the Revolutionary War,
between the Revolutionary and Civil wars, or after the Civil War?

_____

How do you know?

_____
_____

FRIDAY: Book _____
Time _____ Pages _____
Write a summary of today's reading that includes a series of
words separated by commas and a conjunction.

_____
_____

Name _____

READING LOG

MONDAY: Book _____

Time _____ Pages _____

Choose a musical instrument that would provide the best background

accompaniment for today's reading. _____

Explain your choice. _____

_____

_____

TUESDAY: Book _____

Time _____ Pages _____

What plant is your reading today most like? _____

Explain. _____

_____

_____

WEDNESDAY: Book _____

Time _____ Pages _____

Choose three minor characters in the story and rank them on the lines below.

least important _____

somewhat important _____

most important _____

Could the author have left out the least important character?   Yes   No

Explain. _____

_____

_____

THURSDAY: Book _____

Time _____ Pages _____

Humans are curious beings. Identify a character who is curious and tell why.

_____

_____

FRIDAY: Book _____

Time _____ Pages _____

Use a pronoun in a compound subject that tells what you and the main

character have in common. Remember to name yourself last.

_____

_____

Name _____ # READING LOG _____

MONDAY: Book _____

Time _____ Pages _____

What problem might the main character face in a sequel to your story?

_____

_____

How might that character solve the problem?

_____

_____

_____

TUESDAY: Book _____

Time _____ Pages _____

Name a physical or personal trait of the main character shared by other family members.
Give reasons to support your answer.

_____

_____

_____

WEDNESDAY: Book _____

Time _____ Pages _____

In terms of a 24-hour day, how much time has passed in today's story?

_____ days or _____ hours

THURSDAY: Book _____

Time _____ Pages _____

At this point in your story, what event has had the greatest effect on the characters?

Explain your answer. _____

_____

_____

_____

FRIDAY: Book _____

Time _____ Pages _____

Use two adjectives to describe the main character's personality that
also describe you. Find a classmate who agrees with your choices.

1. _____ 2. _____

Classmate's initials _____

Name _____   **READING LOG** ____

MONDAY: Book _____

Time _____ Pages _____

Suppose the main character came to your home for a family dinner.

Where would you wish that person to sit? _____

Explain your reasons. _____

_____

_____

TUESDAY: Book _____

Time _____ Pages _____

Friction creates heat. Oil acts as a lubricant to reduce friction and heat.

Name the source of the friction between two story characters.

Name another character who might act as a lubricant to reduce the friction.

_____

_____

_____

WEDNESDAY: Book _____

Time _____ Pages _____

If $a = 1$, $b = 2$, $c = 3$, and so on,

what is the value of your main character's full name? _____

Show the value of each letter and your calculation on the back of this paper.

THURSDAY: Book _____

Time _____ Pages _____

People constantly interact with their environment. Provide an example

from your story that supports this statement.

_____

_____

FRIDAY: Book _____

Time _____ Pages _____

List four attributes that you want in a best friend.

1. _____   3. _____

2. _____   4. _____

Circle those attributes your main character has.

Do you think that character would be a best friend, a close friend,

or an acquaintance? _____

28

Name _____   # READING LOG _____

MONDAY: Book _____

Time _____   Pages _____

An *appositive* is a word or phrase that tells more about a noun
and is usually set off by commas.
Include an appositive in a one-sentence summary of today's reading.

_____

_____

TUESDAY: Book _____

Time _____   Pages _____

What nonliving thing has affected a character or event in the story?

Explain. _____

_____

_____

WEDNESDAY: Book _____

Time _____   Pages _____

If your neighbor reads 2.8 times faster than you, how many pages would
that person have read today? _____ × 2.8 = _____

     _____   _____
     # pages you read   # pages neighbor read

THURSDAY: Book _____

Time _____   Pages _____

Think of a situation in which the main character acted responsibly or irresponsibly.
Explain what the character did and how you feel about that action.

_____

_____

FRIDAY: Book _____

Time _____   Pages _____

Choose a nursery rhyme that relates to your story.

_____

How are the two related?

_____

_____

_____

Name _____

READING LOG

MONDAY: Book _____

Time _____ Pages _____

Revise the first sentence of your book so it can grab the attention of the next reader.

_____

_____

TUESDAY: Book _____

Time _____ Pages _____

Take the temperature of today's reading in Fahrenheit and Celsius.

_____

Explain your answer.

_____

_____

WEDNESDAY: Book _____

Time _____ Pages _____

Divide the number of letters in the main character's name by the number of vowels in the name.

Name _____

Fraction _____

Is the fraction > or < 1/2? _____

THURSDAY: Book _____

Time _____ Pages _____

Suppose the main character befriended you. Predict how she or he might change you or your environment.

_____

_____

FRIDAY: Book _____

Time _____ Pages _____

Place an X on the line to show how courageous your main character is.

_____

   not courageous   **somewhat courageous**   **very courageous**

Explain your answer. _____

_____

_____

Name _____   # READING LOG ____

MONDAY: Book _____

Time _____ Pages _____

Summarize today's reading in a sentence that describes something a character owns.
Use a possessive noun. (Remember to include an apostrophe.)

_____

_____

TUESDAY: Book _____

Time _____ Pages _____

In what way is a character affected by his or her natural environment?

_____

_____

WEDNESDAY: Book _____

Time _____ Pages _____

In algebra, letters stand for values. Assign a value to each letter in a character's
first name. Then create a multiplication problem for your neighbor to solve.
Check your partner's work.

Example: values for each letter in Kim: K = 8; I = 2; M = 5.
Multiplication problem: KIM × MK = ? (825 × 58 = 47,850)
Work on the back of this paper.

THURSDAY: Book _____

Time _____ Pages _____

Do you think your main character would agree or disagree with the expression
"Never tell a lie"? _____

Explain. _____

_____

_____

FRIDAY: Book _____

Time _____ Pages _____

Suppose an artist wants to illustrate the setting of your story.
Describe what the artist would portray and what medium would be used.

_____

_____

Name _____   # READING LOG _____

MONDAY: Book _____

Time _____ Pages _____

Skim today's reading. What tense of *helping verbs* (such as the verb *is*

in *is walking*) seems to appear most often? _____

Meet in a small group to compare answers. What tense (past, present, future)

is the most common? _____ Least common? _____

TUESDAY: Book _____

Time _____ Pages _____

The nucleus is the control center of a cell.

Who or what is the control center of your story? _____

What kind of control does that character or thing have?

_____

_____

WEDNESDAY: Book _____

Time _____ Pages _____

In algebra, letters stand for values. Assign values to each letter of your author's

last name so that the sum of those letters is greater than 100 but less than 125.

Author's last name _____

Letter values _____

Sum _____

Ask a partner to check your math. Partner's initials _____

THURSDAY: Book _____

Time _____ Pages _____

Identify a problem in the story that would provide material for a public debate.

_____

_____

What expert would you want to judge the debate? _____

Explain your choice. _____

_____

FRIDAY: Book _____

Time _____ Pages _____

To whom would you recommend this book?

_____

Explain. _____

_____

Name _____

READING LOG ____

MONDAY: Book _____
Time _____ Pages _____
Use an *object pronoun* (such as *him, her, it,* or *them*) in a sentence that
describes what happened to a story character in today's reading.

_____

_____

Circle the object pronoun. The pronoun substitutes for what noun? _____

TUESDAY: Book _____
Time _____ Pages _____
Potential energy is a body's capacity for doing work. *Kinetic energy* is a body's
energy in motion. Describe a story character who is demonstrating one of these energies.
Name the character and the kind of energy, then write the description.

_____

_____

WEDNESDAY: Book _____
Time _____ Pages _____
If vowels = $0.05 and consonants = $0.10, what is the value of your book's title?
Show all work.

_____ vowels × $0.05 = _____

_____ consonants × $0.10 = _____

Total value of title = _____

THURSDAY: Book _____
Time _____ Pages _____
Rules and laws are important in a civilization. What rule or law do you notice in your story?

_____
How can you tell?

_____
Is this rule or law an issue in the story or just a part of the characters' lives?

_____

_____

FRIDAY: Book _____
Time _____ Pages _____
Design a logo to represent a character or place in the story.

Name the character or place. _____
Then draw the logo on the back of this paper.
Explain the logo on the lines below.

_____

_____

Name _____ **READING LOG** _____

MONDAY: Book _____

Time _____ Pages _____

Circle the common nouns in your book title above. Put a box around the
proper nouns in the book title. Draw a light line through conjunctions.
Trade papers with a partner. Help each other with any corrections.

Partner's initials _____

TUESDAY: Book _____

Time _____ Pages _____

The walls of plant cells provide protection and support for the plant. Name a character in

your story who provides protection and support. _____

How do you know?

_____

_____

WEDNESDAY: Book _____

Time _____ Pages _____

The total number of pages in your book is _____ .

Write the total in expanded form. _____

_____

THURSDAY: Book _____

Time _____ Pages _____

Letters sometimes contain thanks or requests for help. Name someone to whom the main

character might write for one of those reasons. _____

What might the character write?

_____

_____

FRIDAY: Book _____

Time _____ Pages _____

If the main character came to visit you for the weekend, where would
you take that person on Saturday afternoon?

_____

Why did you choose that place?

_____

_____

READING LOG

Name _____

MONDAY: Book _____

Time _____ Pages _____

Use a comparative adjective to compare the main character to another character in the story. Include reasons why your adjective is accurate.

_____

_____

TUESDAY: Book _____

Time _____ Pages _____

In the laboratory, stains are often added to specimens to make them easier to examine. What object or character in the story would need a "stain" in order to be more easily understandable? _____

Explain. _____

_____

_____

WEDNESDAY: Book _____

Time _____ Pages _____

Suppose your book was reorganized into chapters of 27 pages each. Show the math that tells how many chapters your book would contain.

_____

_____

_____

THURSDAY: Book _____

Time _____ Pages _____

Describe a cause-effect situation involving geography in today's reading.

_____

_____

_____

FRIDAY: Book _____

Time _____ Pages _____

What TV program or movie reminds you of your book? _____
Explain how they are alike.

_____

_____

_____

Name _____

READING LOG _____

MONDAY: Book _____

Time _____ Pages _____

Find a prepositional phrase in today's reading. Include the page number.

_____

Does the phrase tell when, where, how, or to what extent?

_____

TUESDAY: Book _____

Time _____ Pages _____

Waves, currents, and tides cause ocean waters to move. In today's reading, what causes the main character to move?

_____

_____

WEDNESDAY: Book _____

Time _____ Pages _____

Estimate the length, width, and thickness of your book.

Length _____ Width _____ Thickness _____

Use a ruler to check your skill in estimation.

Length _____ Width _____ Thickness _____

You made three estimates. Write a fraction that tells how many were fairly accurate.

_____

THURSDAY: Book _____

Time _____ Pages _____

Agriculture is important to the survival of human life.
Find evidence of agriculture in your story.

_____

_____

FRIDAY: Book _____

Time _____ Pages _____

Mnemonic devices are ways to remember things. Invent a system for remembering the names of four story characters. Teach it to a partner.
Test your partner on Monday.

Characters' names _____

Your system for remembering them

_____

_____

Amount remembered _____

Name _____ # READING LOG _____

MONDAY: Book _____

Time _____ Pages _____

Write a summary sentence that contains an adjective and an adverb.

_____

_____

Circle the adjective and draw a box around the adverb. Draw an
arrow from the adjective and the adverb to the word each modifies.

TUESDAY: Book _____

Time _____ Pages _____

The retina in the eye sends impulses along the optic nerve to the brain.
Describe what your main character sees at the close of today's reading.

_____

_____

How does that image affect him or her?

_____

WEDNESDAY: Book _____

Time _____ Pages _____

Choose a well-described character from the story. _____
Name two pluses about that character.

_____

Name two minuses about that character.

_____

Do you consider the character positive or negative? _____
Explain. _____

_____

THURSDAY: Book _____

Time _____ Pages _____

Major events often cause major changes.
Provide an example from your story that supports this statement.

_____

_____

FRIDAY: Book _____

Time _____ Pages _____

With a partner, discuss the main characters in the books you are reading.
Use a Venn diagram on the back of this paper to compare and contrast the main character
of your book with that of your partner's.

Name _____   # READING LOG

MONDAY: Book _____

Time _____   Pages _____

What *genre*, or type of literature, is your book?

_____

How do you know?

_____

_____

TUESDAY: Book _____

Time _____   Pages _____

Nearsightedness means far-away objects appear blurry. *Farsightedness* means close objects appear blurry. Do you think your main character is more nearsighted or farsighted in understanding the world?

_____

Explain. _____

_____

_____

WEDNESDAY: Book _____

Time _____   Pages _____

Compare the number of pages you read to the amount of time it took.

Approximately how many pages did you read per minute? _____
Use this space to show your work.

THURSDAY: Book _____

Time _____   Pages _____

Name a natural resource in your story. _____
How is it important to the plot?

_____

_____

FRIDAY: Book _____

Time _____   Pages _____

A couplet is a two-line poem that rhymes.
Write a couplet that summarizes today's reading.

_____

_____

Name _____   # READING LOG ___

MONDAY: Book _____
Time _____ Pages _____
Find a paragraph in your story with at least four sentences.
Count the number of words in each sentence.

1. _____   3. _____
2. _____   4. _____

Writers often include sentences of different lengths.
Did your author follow this practice?

_____

TUESDAY: Book _____
Time _____ Pages _____
Which muscles of the body does your main character seem to use most?

_____
For what activities are these muscles used?

_____

WEDNESDAY: Book _____
Time _____ Pages _____
Write an equation using the following words.

_____ + _____ = _____
        character   character/object   problem/solution

THURSDAY: Book _____
Time _____ Pages _____
When people face problems in an environment they can either adapt, alter their
surroundings, or leave. What might your character do to solve his or her problem?

_____

_____

_____

FRIDAY: Book _____
Time _____ Pages _____
Suppose your story is made into a play.
Which character would you choose to be? _____
Explain. _____

_____

_____

Name _____ **READING LOG** ____

MONDAY: Book _____

Time _____ Pages _____

Use the superlative form of an adjective to describe a character from your story.
Use the comparative form of the same adjective to describe two other characters.

_____

Give reasons to support your answer.

_____

_____

TUESDAY: Book _____

Time _____ Pages _____

Your skin surrounds and protects you. What personality traits
does your character use to protect himself or herself?

_____

_____

Explain. _____

_____

_____

WEDNESDAY: Book _____

Time _____ Pages _____

Suppose your character is having a garage sale. Name two items that
person would offer and set a price for each using the dollar sign.

_____

_____

THURSDAY: Book _____

Time _____ Pages _____

What holiday would your character like the least? _____

Explain. _____

_____

_____

FRIDAY: Book _____

Time _____ Pages _____

Would your parent(s) or guardian approve or disapprove

of the main character's actions? _____

Explain. _____

_____

_____

Name _____   # READING LOG   _____

MONDAY: Book _____
Time _____   Pages _____
Describe a "nugget of wisdom" that a character has learned.

_____

_____

TUESDAY: Book _____
Time _____   Pages _____
Coniferous trees are mostly evergreens, and *deciduous trees* shed
leaves and other parts seasonally. Is the main character more like a
coniferous tree or a deciduous tree? _____
Explain. _____

_____

_____

WEDNESDAY: Book _____
Time _____   Pages _____
As you skim three pages of text, count the number of lines in each paragraph.
Do not include one-line dialogues. Find the average.
Show your work on the back of this paper.

THURSDAY: Book _____
Time _____   Pages _____
Social problems such as unemployment or divorce can create difficulties
in families. Identify a problem in the family from which your character comes.
_____
Provide story clues to support your answer.

_____

_____

_____

FRIDAY: Book _____
Time _____   Pages _____
Suppose you can grant wishes. What would be your wish for the main character?
_____
How would your wish change your character's life?

_____

_____

_____

Name _____ **READING LOG** ____

MONDAY: Book _____

Time _____ Pages _____

If your main character were writing an autobiography, what would be the entry for today?

_____

_____

_____

TUESDAY: Book _____

Time _____ Pages _____

Watch your neighbor's eyes as that person describes an event in his or her story. When memory is triggered by pictures in the mind, a right-handed person's eyes tend to shift to about "two o'clock," and a left-handed person's eyes tend to shift to about "ten o'clock." Did your neighbor's eyes shift to either position?

Explain. _____

_____

WEDNESDAY: Book _____

Time _____ Pages _____

There are many kinds of geometric shapes.

Choose the best shape to represent a story character.

Shape _____ Character _____

Explain your answer.

_____

_____

THURSDAY: Book _____

Time _____ Pages _____

A time capsule contains a group of items that represent a particular time and place. Plan a time capsule for the book you are reading. List five things you would gather to represent what life was like for your story's characters.

1. _____ 3. _____ 5. _____

2. _____ 4. _____

FRIDAY: Book _____

Time _____ Pages _____

Photographers can use filters on their lenses to create certain moods. Choose a colored filter to help create the current mood in the story.

What color filter did you choose? _____

Explain. _____

_____

Name _____   REAVING LOG ___

MONDAY: Book _____

Time _____ Pages _____

There are many reading comprehension strategies, including visualizing,
rereading, or using decoding skills. Identify three strategies
you used in today's reading and tell why they were useful.

_____

_____

TUESDAY: Book _____

Time _____ Pages _____

Parasites rely on other organisms for survival. Parasites may harm their hosts.

What character in the story is like a parasite? _____

Explain. _____

_____

WEDNESDAY: Book _____

Time _____ Pages _____

Name characters that fit the circle diagrams below.

Explain. _____

_____

THURSDAY: Book _____

Time _____ Pages _____

If you could shout a message to the main character, what would it be?
(Don't forget the exclamation point!)

_____

What message would you whisper?

_____

FRIDAY: Book _____

Time _____ Pages _____

If the author included dance in the story, what kind would it be? _____

Who would be the dancer? _____

Explain.

_____

Name _____

MONDAY: Book _____

Time _____ Pages _____

Based on your reading today, would you recommend this book to

anyone else? _____ Who? _____

Explain your choice.

_____

_____

_____

TUESDAY: Book _____

Time _____ Pages _____

We often refer to there being a certain "chemistry" between some people.

Choose two characters between whom you feel there is chemistry.

Name them and explain your selection.

_____

_____

_____

WEDNESDAY: Book _____

Time _____ Pages _____

Who is your favorite character from today's reading? _____

Write a fraction that shows in what amount of the pages you

read today this character appeared. _____

Convert your answer to a decimal that shows what percent of your

reading the character appeared in. _____

THURSDAY: Book _____

Time _____ Pages _____

Did the geographic setting of your story have any direct effect on

your reading today? _____ Explain your answer.

_____

_____

_____

FRIDAY: Book _____

Time _____ Pages _____

Choose three words from today's reading that you think are particularly descriptive.

Explain your choices. _____

_____

READING LOG

Name _____

MONDAY: Book _____

Time _____ Pages _____

Choose two characters from today's reading and compare each to an appropriate color. Explain your selections.

_____
_____
_____

TUESDAY: Book _____

Time _____ Pages _____

Choose two different characters from those you chose yesterday and compare each to an appropriate season of the year. Explain your selections.

_____
_____
_____

WEDNESDAY: Book _____

Time _____ Pages _____

What is the sum of all the page numbers you read today? _____

What is the product of the first page number you read and the last one? _____

What is the difference between the number of the last page you read

and the number of the last page of the book? _____

THURSDAY: Book _____

Time _____ Pages _____

What emotions might your characters have experienced in today's reading?

_____

Choose one character/emotion and explain its importance to the story.

_____
_____

FRIDAY: Book _____

Time _____ Pages _____

Would your story make a good movie? _____
Explain your answer.

_____
_____
_____

Rating Responses to Prompts

To rate student responses on the log sheets, specific criteria should be established and conveyed to students. In "Getting Started" we identified three labels to use when assessing student work. Here are possible criteria for each label.

Powerful
- strong evidence of thoughtfulness
- clear, concise, and specific
- sentence form

Satisfactory
- some evidence of thoughtfulness
- somewhat clear, concise, and specific
- sentence form

Inadequate
- little evidence of thoughtfulness
- unclear, disorganized, and nonspecific
- not sentence form

You may wish to use this criteria to assess student responses. If a student does not use the sentence form when required, the response is labeled *inadequate*. To be labeled *powerful* a response must meet all three criteria. If one of the first two criteria under *powerful* is not met, the response is then checked against *satisfactory* criteria. If either of those first two criteria is not met, the response is rated *inadequate*. By demonstrating the assessment process using the think-aloud approach, students will learn to recognize the appropriate rating for most responses. Being consistent and measuring by the criteria are the most important guidelines.

Consider the following five sample responses to the following prompt:

If the main character visited our classroom for one day, which student would be an appropriate partner for that person? _____
Explain. _____
_____

1. Who? James
   Explain. James and Jonas are both boys. _____

2. Who? Nina
   Explain. Nina and Jonas have a keen sense of adventure and like to make their own decisions. _____

3. Who? Lin
   Explain. to keep each other company _____

4. Who? Cindy
   Explain. She likes to meet new people. _____

5. Who? Georgio
   Explain. Both boys want the same things. _____

Using the criteria found on the previous page rate each of the sample responses, compare your ratings to ours:

1. **inadequate** (There is little evidence of thoughtfulness.)

2. **powerful**

3. **inadequate** (The response is not in sentence form.)

4. **satisfactory** (There is some evidence of thoughtfulness but no specifics.)

5. **satisfactory** (It lacks specifics.)

Are you doing something wrong if your ratings do not match ours? Not at all. You are simply applying the criteria as you interpret them. The key point is to establish criteria and demonstrate your interpretation of that criteria for students so they understand your method of assessment.